Meet **Desert** ANIMALS

Pebble® Plus

KANGAROOS

by **Rose Davin**

CAPSTONE PRESS
a capstone imprint

Pebble Plus is published by Capstone Press,
1710 Roe Crest Drive, North Mankato, Minnesota 56003
www.mycapstone.com

Library of Congress Cataloging-in-Publication Data
Names: Davin, Rose, author.
Title: Kangaroos / by Rose Davin.
Description: North Mankato, Minnesota : Capstone Press, [2017] | Series: Pebble
plus. Meet desert animals | Audience: Ages 4–8. | Audience: K to grade 3. | Includes
bibliographical references and index.
Identifiers: LCCN 2016035494 | ISBN 9781515746041 (library binding) | ISBN
  9781515746119 (pbk.) | ISBN 9781515746294 (eBook PDF)
Subjects: LCSH: Kangaroos—Juvenile literature.
Classification: LCC QL737.M35 D38 2017 | DDC 599.2/22—dc23
LC record available at https://lccn.loc.gov/2016035494

Editorial Credits
Marysa Storm and Alesha Sullivan, editors; Kayla Rossow, designer;
Ruth Smith, media researcher; Kathy McColley, production specialist

Photo Credits
Ardea: © Jean-Paul Ferrero, 21; Capstone Press: 6; naturepl.com: Rolan Seitre, 15;
Shutterstock: Christopher Meder, 1, Asian Images, 2, 24, Ilia Torlin, 7, John Carnemolla,
cover, back cover, 5, K.A.Willis, 17, Karel Gallas, 13, Kjuuurs, 24, mark higgins, 9,
optionm, 22, Rafael Ramirez Lee, 11, Warren Field, 19

Note to Parents and Teachers

The Meet Desert Animals set supports national curriculum standards for science
related to life science and ecosystems. This book describes and illustrates kangaroos.
The images support early readers in understanding the text. The repetition of words
and phrases helps early readers learn new words. This book also introduces early
readers to subject-specific vocabulary words, which are defined in the Glossary
section. Early readers may need assistance to read some words and to use the Table of
Contents, Glossary, Read More, Internet Sites, Critical Thinking Using the Common
Core, and Index sections of the book.

Printed and bound in China.
007872

TABLE OF CONTENTS

HIGH HOPPERS

Hop! A kangaroo jumps in the air.

It hops on its big hind feet.

A kangaroo's strong tail helps it

move and stand.

Kangaroos live in Australia and
on nearby islands. They live in deserts,
woodlands, and grasslands.
Some kangaroos live in groups called mobs.

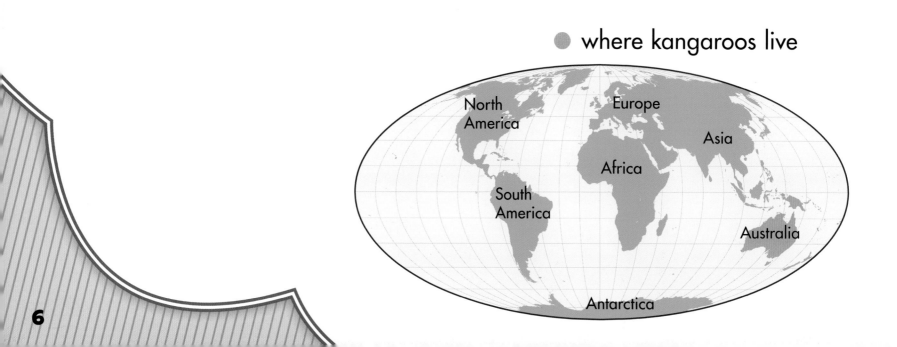

● where kangaroos live

North America
Europe
Asia
Africa
South America
Australia
Antarctica

BIG AND SMALL

Some kangaroos are big. They weigh about 200 pounds (91 kilograms). Others are little. They weigh only 12 ounces (340 grams).

Kangaroos have brown, gray, or red fur.

They have strong back legs with big feet.

Their front legs are short.

TIME TO EAT

Kangaroos eat at night.

They munch on grass, leaves, and shrubs.

LIFE CYCLE

A female kangaroo usually has

one baby at a time.

Kangaroo babies are called joeys.

Newborn joeys are hairless.

They are about 1 inch (2.5 centimeters) long.

Joeys grow in their mothers' pouches.

They drink their mothers' milk.

Older joeys go in and out of the pouches.

Cluck! Kangaroo mothers call to their

joeys to keep them near.

Kangaroos listen for danger with their big ears.

They pound their feet on the ground.

This warns the mob of danger.

Wild dogs called dingoes attack kangaroos. Kangaroos fight these predators with their hind feet. Kangaroos can live about 8 years in the wild.

Glossary

desert—an area of dry land with few plants; deserts receive little rain

grassland—open land covered mostly with grass

island—a piece of land that is surrounded by water

mob—a group of kangaroos that lives together; each mob has up to 20 kangaroos

pouch—a flap of skin that looks like a pocket in which some animals carry their young; young kangaroos live in the pouches after they are born

predator—an animal that hunts other animals for food

woodland—land that is covered by trees and shrubs

Read More

Calhoun, Kelly. *High-Speed Hoppers.* Guess What. Ann Arbor, Mich.: Cherry Lake Publishing, 2016.

Ganeri, Anita. *The Story of the Kangaroo.* Fabulous Animals. Chicago: Capstone, 2016.

Saxby, Claire. *Big Red Kangaroo.* Somerville, Mass.: Candlewick Press, 2015.

Internet Sites

FactHound offers a safe, fun way to find Internet sites related to this book. All of the sites on FactHound have been researched by our staff.

Here's all you do:

Visit *www.facthound.com*

Type in this code: 9781515746041

Super-cool stuff!

Check out projects, games and lots more at
www.capstonekids.com

Critical Thinking Using the Common Core

1. How do you think pouches help keep joeys safe? (Integration of Knowledge and Ideas)

2. Why are big ears helpful to a kangaroo? (Key Ideas and Details)

3. In what ways are kangaroos social animals? How might this be helpful? (Integration of Knowledge and Ideas)

Index